RECLAIM
a Generation

21 DAYS OF PRAYER
FOR SCHOOLS

CHERYL SACKS

BRIDGEBUILDERS
INT'L LEADERSHIP NETWORK

PRAYERSHOP
PUBLISHING

Terre Haute, Indiana

PrayerShop Publishing is the publishing arm of the Church Prayer Leaders Network. The Church Prayer Leaders Network exists to equip and inspire local churches and their prayer leaders in their desire to disciple their people in prayer and to become a "house of prayer for all nations." Its online store, prayershop.org, has more than 150 prayer resources available for purchase or download.

ISBN (Print): 978-1-970176-19-3
ISBN (E-Book): 978-1-970176-20-9

TABLE OF CONTENTS

WEEK 3: Spiritual Awakening: Preparing the Way for Hope, Healing, and Freedom | 49

APPENDIX

INTRODUCTION

The Lord has a great plan for this emerging generation—they will take the gospel into every sphere of influence and contend for the cultural keys to our nation, bringing reformation and revival to the land. At the same time, our Enemy is actively at work, strategizing how he can destroy our children. Just as he sought to destroy Joseph, Moses, and Jesus, he wants to stop this young generation from fulfilling God's call on their lives.

One of our greatest callings as the Church is to stand in the gap for our children. God, in fact, looks for people who will step up in this way: "And I sought for a man among them who should build up the wall and stand in the breach (gap) before me for the land . . ." (Ezek. 22:30, ESV).

You and I, as godly parents and leaders, and members of Christ's Kingdom, must both raise up the next generation in God's Truth and come alongside them in fervent prayer—standing in the gap to defeat hopelessness, addictions, discouragement, and perversion. We are in a spiritual fight for the hearts and minds of our children.

It's time for us to stand with this generation in their life's battles, interceding for the preservation of their destinies. It is time to reclaim a generation! This prayer guide is designed to give you hope, and inspire your prayers, as together we hold up the emerging generation before Almighty God, the Faithful One, whose name is above every name in heaven and earth. We can pray with the psalmist, "Let God arise, and the enemies of our children be scattered" (Psalm 68:1, paraphrased)!

We hope you will use this 21-Day Prayer Guide, *Reclaim a Generation,* to pray for the schools in your community, or for the schools of children you care about that might not be in your own city. If possible, put "boots on the ground" and get out onto your school campuses and prayerwalk the property. Parents and kids can pray. Grandparents can pray. Neighbors can pray. Your group can comprise as many—or as few—intercessors as you like.

Scripture tells us that "the earnest prayer of a righteous person has great power and produces wonderful results" (James 5:16b, NLT). Our prayers matter. *Your* prayers matter. Through prayer, we can reclaim a generation from the Enemy's efforts to sow fear, deception, and disunity. Through prayer, we can invite God's Holy Spirit onto our school campuses. Through prayer, we can exercise our authority in Christ, and declare and release God's power over the lives of our students, launching them into their God-given destinies.

Thank you for standing in the gap for the next generation,

Cheryl Sacks

WEEK 1

STUDENT LIFE

Excelling in Studies and Growing in Godly Character

Day 1: EXCELLENCE IN ACADEMICS

Choose my instruction instead of silver,
knowledge rather than choice gold,
for wisdom is more precious than rubies, and
nothing you desire can compare with her. . .
I love those who love me, and those who seek me find me.
With me are riches and honor, enduring
wealth and prosperity. . .
(PROVERBS 8:10-12, 17-18, NIV)

The students of today are the leaders of tomorrow. Of course, we hope and pray that the future leaders being educated in our nation's schools, and released into our communities to serve and lead, will be well-equipped for the task. Alarmingly, when one looks deeply into the matter, we find many reports telling us the opposite.

The U.S. Department of Education reports that the high school graduation rate is at an all-time high at 80 percent. Four out of five learners, they say, are successful in studies completion and graduate within four years. While these statistics may sound promising at first glance, they are overshadowed by the literacy rate in the United States. While 80 percent of high school seniors obtain a diploma, demonstrably less than half can proficiently read or even complete math problems. Fifty-four (54) percent of U.S. adults 16 to 74 years old—about 130 million people—lack proficiency in literacy, reading below the equivalent of a sixth-grade level.[1]

---

1. https://www.forbes.com/sites/michaeltnietzel/2020/09/09/low-literacy
-levels-among-us-adults-could-be-costing-the-economy-22-trillion-a
-year/. Accessed 27 February 2022.

So, on closer examination, it becomes evident that while 80 percent of today's students are technically graduating from their high schools, less than half of them are prepared for what's next.

It seems that students are being socially promoted when they should be held back and repeating work they have not mastered. As they are moved ahead without demonstrating mastery, these students are at a distinct disadvantage: they cannot complete grade-level work and keep up with their classmates. They have a heightened chance of falling behind and dropping out of high school or college.

Many critics of the system believe that the major problem with public education in America today is a lack of focus on results. Students are simply no longer expected to meet high standards.

We know these concerns run the entire spectrum of our education system. Let's stand in agreement for a spirit of excellence to fall on every student in our public, private, and home schools, and in our universities, that they may reach their full potential and fulfill the destinies God has for them.

Let's Pray

Father, we lift before You the schools across our nation, from kindergartens to universities. We pray they would adhere to high standards that will properly equip students for their next steps in career and in life:

- We pray Proverbs 8:1-21 over our students. God, make their time in the classroom count—may You maximize their time and impart supernatural wisdom. Your Word says that with wisdom comes good judgment, knowledge, discernment, common sense, insight, strength, and success.

- We ask that You pour out a love of learning and a hunger for knowledge, and ignite in our students a drive for academic success. Give them a deep desire to seek godly wisdom and its blessings. We pray they will value their education and be so motivated that they would let nothing stand in the way of graduating! May they be lifelong learners who excel in their respective fields.

- We will trust You for fresh, innovative solutions *from heaven* at both the state and local levels in how to raise our graduation rates and increase competency in academics. We need future leaders who are well-equipped for the task. May we educate and equip our students in a way that empowers them to thrive.

Day 2: TRUTH IN CURRICULA

*Be careful not to let anyone rob you of this faith
through a shallow and misleading philosophy. Such
a person follows human traditions and the world's
way of doing things rather than following Christ.*
(COLOSSIANS 2:8, GOD'S WORD)

*"The education of youth should be watched
with the most scrupulous attention. . .
[It] lays the foundations on which both
law and gospel rest for success."*
—NOAH WEBSTER, WELL-KNOWN AMERICAN EDUCATOR

Research shows that now, more than ever, moral convictions are waning in today's society. Many, if not most, textbooks have been drastically revised to present a new view of American and world history, and the history of humanity. The founding of our country is being reframed by those who would want to present it as rooted in exploitation, instead of the victorious expression of God-given freedom and liberty that true history demonstrates.

Science is presented as a system of knowledge that excludes God. Evolution is taught as fact in public schools, even though, at the end his life, Darwin denounced his own theories. Neither science nor the history textbooks mention this important detail! Fewer and fewer Americans believe in a clear and distinct right or wrong, and often our public schools are reinforcing these "new norms" as progressive and just.

Additionally, through sex education classes, children as young as elementary-aged are being taught about marriage, identity, and sexuality "norms" that are outside of God's biblical plan for us. As our country leans more and more into moral relativism, students are learning in schools that morality is up to them to decide.

In the last few years, the assault on truth has escalated. Parents across the nation have risen up to reclaim truth in their school districts. As the praying church, we need to stand united! We must pray for our children, our teachers, and our school boards, that these destructive agendas do not make their way into the curricula of our local schools.

May our Christian students stand firm in their convictions, and may they be a light to those who do not believe, pointing them to God's righteousness.

Let's Pray

Lord, we ask that You shine Your light upon our schools and drive out all darkness, spiritual blindness, perversion of truth, and hostility toward You and Your truth.

- We pray that all attempts to use curricula in our schools as a way to disciple our young people in humanism, moral relativism, and other godless ideologies would be stopped. We pray that our education system would honor You.
- We ask You to raise up godly men and women to be on textbook selection committees for every school district in our nation. We ask for teachers and school boards to select curriculum that preserves our godly heritage as a nation.

- Lord, we ask that You lead and guide those in positions of decision-making in our schools to set fair policies that protect the rights of our teachers and students to openly present their biblical points of view in an open, fair, and non-threatening manner.
- Father, when teachers and students are confronted with subject matter that goes against their biblical worldview, we call upon You to give them the right words to speak with wisdom, strength, and gentleness.
- Raise up watchmen and gatekeepers for truth and excellence in our schools who would guard over what is taught to our young people!

Day 3: PHYSICAL HEALTH AND SAFETY

Beloved, I pray that in all respects you
may prosper and be in good health,
just as your soul prospers.
(3 JOHN 1:2, NASB)

Your bodies are temples of the Holy Spirit
. . . honor God with your bodies.
(1 CORINTHIANS 6:19-20, NIV)

The youth of our nation face a health crisis of epic proportions, including things like alcohol and drug abuse, sex and STDs, obesity, and depression. Marijuana use is ever increasing; some states are legalizing marijuana and even though it is still illegal under the age of 21, commercial enterprises are targeting youth in their marketing efforts. Marijuana use among teens in high school is rampant.

Today's children face threats of violence never before seen in this country. Shootings—even the unthinkable horror of school shootings—riots, beatings, and more fill our news headlines, bringing fear and apprehension to many. *Is this world even safe for my babies?* many parents wonder.

On top of this, every student across the nation has been living through a global pandemic for the last two to three years! Most people—parents and students alike—are faced with the decision of whether or not to take the new vaccines being promoted. This raises myriad health concerns, ranging from physical, mental, and emotional.

Jesus, make a way!

Let's Pray

Father, we pray for the physical health, well-being, and safety of all our students.

- We ask that, as our Divine Physician, You would protect our students, heal the ones battling sickness or disease, and release them from any and all forms of addiction in Jesus' name!
- We pray that families would be equipped to disciple youth in a godly way, imparting practical wisdom that leads to a healthy lifestyle. Transform the health of entire households, starting with the parents and filtering down to the students! Please inspire a real change in eating and exercise habits, and help our students be nourished with wholesome food.
- We declare, in Jesus' name, that our campuses are safe from illnesses, and specifically the COVID-19 virus and its variants. We pray that the pandemic would not affect or influence their health, safety, and peace of mind. We ask You to set up a hedge of protection in the spiritual realm that would result in havens of safety and health for the students in our state.
- May Your hand of wisdom rest on every student and parent as they grapple with the decision of whether or not to take the COVID-19 vaccine, if they have not made this decision already,

or its boosters. May each family make a decision that aligns with how Your Spirit is guiding them. We pray against a culture of pressure or divisiveness in our schools about this issue.

- We call on You for an end to the pervasive drug culture in our schools. Please protect our children and young people from getting involved in gangs, drugs, sex, and other destructive activities.

- God, we also pray You would keep our school campuses safe from anyone with ill intent who would seek to bring harm through shooting or other forms of terror and violence. Equip every school with frontline workers who would have eyes out for "wolves" who would in any way harm the students.

Day 4: EMOTIONAL HEALTH AND WELL-BEING

. . . casting all your anxieties on him, because he cares for you.
(1 PETER 5:7, ESV)

*Dear friend, I pray that you may enjoy good health
and that all may go well with you, even
as your soul is getting along well.*
(3 JOHN 1:2, NIV)

According to the National Institutes of Health, nearly one third of all adolescents ages 13 to 18 will experience an anxiety disorder, and these numbers have been rising steadily. While there are a number of factors that are likely contributing to student anxiety, one that stands out as particularly noteworthy is the increased influence of social media.

Today's children and teens are connected constantly to social media and are being bombarded by all kinds of negative messaging.

The resulting anxiety has been undeniable. While it is a great way to communicate through distance, take attractive photos, and stay in touch with loved ones, its abuse is rampant.

Social media platforms are frequently cesspools of bullying, comparison, provocation, and darkness. Studies show that social media does more harm than good—it's not good for anyone's mental or emotional health. It lowers self-esteem, encourages comparison, and paints an unrealistic picture of reality.

We must pray against all the ways social media tells our youth that they are not good enough. Our children must know their worth is unquestionable, despite the messages they are receiving from social media. We must pray against the ways these platforms have destroyed their self-esteem, and ask that God renews their mental and emotional well-being with His divine presence in their lives.

Let's Pray

Lord, we pray for the emotional and mental well-being of our students, knowing that every day they face pressures from others, as well as from what they see online, in the news, or on their smart phone.

- We ask that any messages that inspire fear or lower their self-esteem and their self-worth be replaced with Your unceasing acceptance of them and love for them. May they always know that their worth is unchanging! They are special, with an original design and plan for their life!
- We pray against all the ways social media can be a toxic weapon in the lives of our children and teens. We pray against the spirits of comparison, jealousy, and greed that have robbed them of their youth and innocence. We pray against the ways cyber bullying and mean-spirited online interactions have allowed fear, inadequacy, isolation, and rejection to fester.

- In Jesus' name, we declare that the mental and emotional well-being of our students will not be defined by what others say about them, nor will it be defined by what they think of themselves! We declare contentment, confidence, self-love, generosity, kindness, and joy over the lives of today's youth. We ask that students have the boldness to step away from social media when they know it is harmful, even when it is not the popular choice to do so.

Day 5: STUDENT RELATIONSHIPS

Flee the evil desires of youth and pursue
righteousness, faith, love and peace, along with
those who call on the Lord out of a pure heart.
(2 TIMOTHY 2:22, NIV)

Whoever would foster love covers over an offense,
but whoever repeats the matter separates close friends.
(PROVERBS 17:9, NIV)

Do not be misled: "Bad company corrupts good character."
(1 CORINTHIANS 15:33, NIV)

School relationships can be among the most life-giving or the most damaging in a person's life. From romantic relationships to hierarchical "pecking orders" to racial dynamics and beyond, there is great opportunity for learning—and great opportunity for abuse.

Bullying has become a huge problem in schools, including "cyber bullying," so much so that some students have even felt driven to take their own lives.

The kinds of friends a person chooses in school can set the course for the rest of their life. It is said that a person actually becomes like the three to five people they spend the most time with. Choosing friend groups is a huge part of what will make or break student success and relationships.

Because teachers and support staff cannot be everywhere and monitor everyone, students are often on their own to navigate these areas of socializing in schools. We can ask God to protect students from damaging relationships. We can pray for their minds to be open to God's truths about friendship, love, and marriage, and the value of every human life. We can pray they learn to seek understanding and unity with others who may be different from them, for whatever reason.

To the extent that teachers and curricula are involved in shaping young people's minds, we can pray that there would be alignment with God's heart and will. As young adults are experimenting with new ideas, values, and behaviors, we pray they will be turned away from relationships and interactions that are damaging and hurtful to themselves and others.

Let's Pray

Lord, we lift up our students of all ages to you, asking for Your help, guidance, protection, discernment, and grace as they navigate the sometimes precarious minefield of human relationships.

- We pray for a spirit of inclusiveness that would help our children respect, honor, and accept all people based on the fact that we are all made in Your image, no matter where we come from, what we look like, or any other factor. You love us all unconditionally; help our children to experience and extend that love to one another.
- We boldly come against the vindictive behavior of bullying. We pray that there would be a change in the culture that feeds

this maliciousness. As part of that culture change, we ask that You make Your people shine! Let Christians be known as courageous student champions who defend victims and can bring healing and peace into a situation. Help them to be inclusive with one another, so no one feels "left out." We pray for those who feel alone, help them to find healthy relationships and feel a part of a company of friends.

- As our great Defender, we ask that You shield Christian students and teachers from those who would seek to bully, intimidate, or silence them. We ask that You raise up many who are not ashamed of the gospel and who will exercise their rights to freedom of speech and freedom of religion with boldness and graciousness.

- We pray against the sexualization of our children and the constant messaging from media that they need a romantic relationship to feel accepted. We pray against sexual harassment and every form of sexual innuendo, immorality, and abuse in our schools.

- Holy Spirit, lead our children into choosing positive, healthy relationships in friends and in dating. We pray they will have an inclusive mentality that refuses to shut out those who may be different from them, and that honors everyone from all races and walks of life.

- Raise up strong and godly leadership among Christian groups and campus clubs, we pray, and help them minister effectively to those around them. As the gospel advances on campuses, may the culture shift to one of love, respect, joy, and peace among all students.

Day 6: GENDER AND SEXUALITY

So God created mankind in his own image,
in the image of God he created them;
male and female he created them.
(GENESIS 1:27, NIV)

Sexuality, once an educational responsibility of parents, has moved not just into the mainstream of education, but to the *ex*treme. Not only are today's students being exposed to extremely graphic sexually themed material in some districts, in the name of "sex ed," but they are also being exposed to pressure to accept and embrace transgenderism.

Some schools have been bringing in "Drag Queens" to teach students about alternative lifestyles, calling them "models of diversity." These individuals teach, entertain, and educate kids about being transgender. There are LGBTQ+ curriculums being written and taught in public schools across the nation, and one program has come to be known as "Drag Queen Story Hour."[2]

According to Intercessors for America, as reported in *US News* on January 28, 2022, at a middle school in Massachusetts, the school principal allowed her staff members to meet secretly with an 11-year-old girl interested in becoming a boy and her 12-year-old brother interested in becoming a girl. A teacher who knew the parents notified them immediately. The parents then notified the school principal of their disapproval. The school principal defended the counseling sessions but *fired the teacher* immediately for violating the privacy rights of the minor students by alerting the students' parents.

Another incident at a middle school in California involved two teachers who stalked students online to help identify students they felt would "benefit" from attending the school's LGBTQ club. They

2. https://www.parentsrightsined.org/drag-queen-ed.html. Accessed 27 February 2022.

recruited a 12-year-old student without telling the student's parents. The punishment for the two teachers equated to a minor hand slap. The teachers who used the internet to find vulnerable children to mentor into becoming transgender *did not lose their jobs or suffer suspension* even after parents brought the issue to the school board's attention.

The angry parents in these situations have learned that punishment evades public school perpetrators because powerful institutions support them in their immorality—the U.S. Department of Education and the National Education Association are two chief supporters of this ideology. These organizations provide tools for teachers, counselors, and administrators to assist students with gender transition. In reality, many times they are the ones actually seeding the confusion, through counseling sessions that encourage children to question their gender, all without the parents' knowledge or consent.

Moreover, there is a growing movement afoot to provide "Transition Closets" in schools, where children, according to one teacher who supports the program, ". . . come to school wearing the clothes their parents approve of, and then swap out into the clothes that fit who they 'truly are.'"[3]

The U.S. Department of Education also provides major support of LGBTQ issues in public schools. The U.S. DOE secured COVID-19 money and distributed the money to the states under a program called the American Rescue Plan Elementary and Secondary School Emergency Relief (ARP ESSER). A significant portion of the $122 billion is designated for "mental health support," including guidelines for lending assistance to specifically Lesbian, Gay, Bisexual, Transgender, Queer, or Questioning (LGBTQ2+) youth.[4]

---

3. https://dailyusmagazine.com/politics/schools-using-transition-closets -to-hide-childrens-transgender-identity-from-parents/. Accessed 27 February 2022.
4. https://www.glsen.org/sites/default/files/2021-11/2021-Fall_CSSO -Letter_COVID-19-Relief.pdf. Accessed 27 February 2022.

Sex education has been radically transformed in the last handful of years, morphing from talking about contraception and how to prevent sexually transmitted diseases (STD), to teaching kids how to engage in all kinds of sexual behavior. Parents in some states became distraught when they learned about the sexually explicit sex education instruction being offered to their children. Only recently, when COVID-19 forced students into online-only instruction, did some parents learn that today's sex education in their state has gone way past the "facts of life."

It is no surprise that student sexual activity, pregnancies, pornography use, STDs, gender dysphoria (confusion about sexual identity), and homosexuality continue to explode among our young people. It is probably fair to say this is the most sexually confused and conflicted generation our society has ever seen.

Our students are being pressured into sexual activity at younger and younger ages, by peers, the culture and media, and now even by the schools themselves as these graphic sex ed courses push their way into more and more districts. Our children need our prayers for protection and purity, and the preservation of their innocence. Schoolteachers and administrators need wisdom and courage to push back against immoral guidelines and curriculum that promote these ideologies and behaviors. Legislators, too, need wisdom and courage to prevail when legislation comes through asking for a vote on promoting these programs.

Let's Pray

Lord, we recognize we do not battle against mere flesh and blood, but against spiritual powers in heavenly places. There is a spiritual agenda to destroy the innocence and purity of our children, and to corrupt them and lead them down the wrong path with regard to their God-given sexuality and identity.

- God, as we face these enemy forces that would lead our students into sexual sin, we declare that You have promised to preserve the godly inheritance of parents and our nation—and that heritage is our children.

- We take authority in Jesus' name over every wicked spirit that brings these messages of corruption, perversion, and immorality to our precious children. This day, we ask for Your deliverance for our schools and our children from these enemy forces.

- We pray these graphic sexual curriculums would not be approved for use in our schools, that these "clubs" that promote perverted ideologies would be canceled and prohibited, and that teachers with activist agendas to corrupt our youth would be exposed and expelled, in Jesus' name.

- We pray that laws for curriculum transparency would be enacted in every state. We pray that teachers, school boards, administrators, and counselors would be required (and held accountable) to notify parents regarding surveys offered to students, books to be read, or speakers that will be coming in. We pray all deception and efforts made in secrecy to influence and corrupt our children would be exposed and brought into the light, in Jesus' name (see Matt. 10:26; Luke 12:2).

- Lord, we pray for our children, that Your Spirit would fill them with a desire and value for purity. Help them to stand strong against peer pressure and the lies of the enemy and our culture. Give them courage and strength not to give into temptation, but to look for and seize the way of escape that You always provide.

Day 7: OVERCOMING ADVERSITY

Say no to wrong. Learn to do good. Work
for justice. Help the down-and-out.
Stand up for the homeless. Go to bat for the defenseless.
(ISAIAH 1:17, MSG)

God can pour on the blessings in astonishing ways
so that you're ready for anything and everything,
more than just ready to do what needs to be done.
(2 CORINTHIANS 9:8, MSG)

"Vision is the #1 predictor of success in school.
It's much more predictive than test scores."
JOHN HUPPENTHAL, FORMER ARIZONA
SUPERINTENDENT OF PUBLIC INSTRUCTION

Many schools are overwhelmed with helping students who may require additional help due to their home circumstances, such as lack of parental presence or support, or poverty. They may be immigrants or refugees from different parts of the world. Many of these students have never been in a school and are struggling to grasp a new language in addition to their own. Teachers face an enormous challenge in trying to include and educate children from such a variation of educational backgrounds and families of origin.

Across the nation, there are schools facing these issues. We know that obstacles such as poverty, lack of access to transportation, addiction and substance abuse within the home, broken families, depression and other mental illness, generational curses, familial expectations and norms, undiagnosed learning disabilities, racial inequality, homelessness and more, can all be mitigating factors in the academic success of any student. However, God, through His supernatural power, can make a way!

Let's Pray

Father, Your Word tells us that without a vision people perish (Proverbs 29:18).

- Lord, we pray for VISION for administrators, principals, teachers, parents, and students! Give them Your vision of what their schools can become and stir their faith and hope to action. Let them see that NOTHING is impossible with God, no matter how bad the situation!
- Father of Light, we ask You to plant a vision within our students to see academic success as a real possibility in their lives. Give them a vision to overcome the challenges they live with.
- We pray for mentors and tutors to come alongside each one who is struggling and give them the educational support and vital encouragement needed to finish their schooling.
- Please open the windows of heaven over our struggling schools: for finances and good staff, that they would receive a blessing they can't contain! Lord, we ask that You would be glorified when their needs are supernaturally met.
- Help our students who are struggling—whether with learning disabilities or with troubled families or anything else that would hinder them. We pray that You would restore their confidence and motivation, that failures and setbacks would not discourage them. And we ask that You release the specialized teachers these students need.
- Encourage all who feel like giving up to press through to victory!

WEEK 2

STUDENT SUPPORT SYSTEMS

Home, School, Community, and Church

Day 8: TAKING GROUND: RECLAIMING TRUTH AND VALUES

*"So justice is driven back, and righteousness
stands at a distance; truth has stumbled in
the streets, honesty cannot enter."*
(ISAIAH 59:14, NIV)

*"Then you will know the truth, and
the truth will set you free."*
(JOHN 8:32, NIV)

This week, we will pray for the support systems that instill truth and values in our students, as well as provide for their academic instruction and social/emotional learning and growth.

Truth, in our culture, is under assault. In fact, it has been said, in the face of the constant barrage of untruths and half-truths that have infiltrated and dominated our news, schools, entertainment, and academia in recent years, that we actually live in a "post-truth era." Does this mean the truth has been mysteriously lost, and that it cannot be found? Of course not. It does mean that the truth must be sought out and contended for like never before.

Our children are our most vulnerable population when it comes to the truth. They are dependent upon us to protect their minds and hearts from that which would direct their spirits and intellects away from the Lord and toward ungodly and destructive philosophies and worldviews. No longer can we simply trust the instructions and systems in our nation to teach the objective and defensible truth, and godly values, to our children (or to anyone, really). We must be on the alert, practically and spiritually.

We pray our younger generation will be like Daniel, who, when he found himself in a culture hostile to biblical truth and godly values, "resolved not to eat the king's food." Though it was appealing, Daniel knew it wasn't good for him and his companions—and after refusing it, they emerged from their training healthier and stronger than all the other young men! This resolve marked Daniel throughout his life, and propelled him to the highest levels of leadership.

Let's Pray

Father, thank You for Jesus' promise that the truth will set us free. We pray for our children, that You will place people around them who will help them walk in the truth; Your Word is truth!

- We pray for teachers and parents, Father: for discernment to recognize deception and false ideologies, and the faith and courage to push back against the sources and fight for truth.
- We, also, pray for administrators and school board members, that they would be gatekeepers of truth in their school districts, and that the lies of the enemy would not get past them. Put godly people in these positions, Lord, to serve Your purposes and defend Your truth in our classrooms.
- We declare that the efforts of those who are trying to create curricula and initiatives in our schools to actively promote lies and anti-God philosophies and activities will be thwarted and defeated at every turn.
- We ask that You increase discernment, Lord, in even the youngest of students, and that they would learn to correctly handle and apply the Word of Truth (2 Timothy 2:15) to everything they learn, no matter what the subject matter is.
- We proclaim, in the powerful name of Jesus, that this generation will rise up as warriors for truth, take back the ground

the enemy has stolen, and reclaim their godly heritage in our nation!

Day 9: HOME LIFE

He will turn the hearts of the parents to their children,
and the hearts of the children to their parents; or else I
will come and strike the land with total destruction.
(MALACHI 4:6, NIV)

Fathers, do not exasperate your children; instead,
bring them up in the training and instruction of the Lord.
(EPHESIANS 6:4, NIV)

Families are the cornerstone of our society, and the frontline support system for students. Where this support system is strong, our children thrive. Where it is weak, they struggle. Unfortunately, many families are under immense pressure from poverty, homelessness, lack of secure employment, and the challenges of single parenting.

Nearly 11 million children are living in poverty in America, according to a report from January of 2021. More than 4 in 10 children live in a household struggling to meet basic expenses, and between 7 to 11 million children live in households in which they are unable to eat enough because of the cost of food.[5]

Across the nation, states identified 1,280,866 students experiencing homelessness during the school year 2019-2020.[6] Without stable housing, young people are more vulnerable to mental health problems, developmental delays, and poor cognitive outcomes.

---

5. Haider, Areeba. "The Basic Facts about Children in Poverty." *American-Progress.org.* January 12, 2021. Accessed 27 February 2022.
6. https://www.nche.ed.gov/wp-content/uploads/2021/12/Student
-Homelessness-in-America-2021.pdf. Accessed 27 February 2022.

Further, there is a correlation between housing instability and trauma, which can negatively impact future success. Educational outcomes for children are also improved with housing stability. Young people in stable housing are less likely to repeat a grade and less likely to drop out of school. Ultimately, the lack of stable housing has long-lasting effects that can impact health, education, and employment throughout people's lives and in future generations.[7]

The challenges of single-parent households can also deeply affect children; in 2017, 25 percent of U.S. households were headed by a single parent. As of 2019, there were 15.76 million children living with their single mothers in the United States. In the same year, 3.23 million children were living with their single fathers.[8]

We can add to the above challenges other issues such as drug and alcohol abuse, marital tensions/divorce, and domestic violence. Many families are still recovering from the economic and social-emotional challenges of the COVID-19 pandemic. Our students' households need our prayers more than ever!

Let's Pray

Father, we thank You for what You are doing in families today.

- We bring before You every family struggling and in pain, whether from divorce, poverty, unemployment, drug or alcohol abuse, or domestic violence. Bring healing, comfort, and provision for these broken and hurting homes.
- Lord, we lift up to You students who are homeless and are staying at shelters, on the street, or living in cars. Your Father's heart

---

7. https://www.usich.gov/resources/uploads/asset_library/Housing -Affordability-and-Stablility-Brief.pdf. Accessed 27 February 2022.
8. https://comparecamp.com/single-parent-statistics/. Accessed 27 February 2022.

is for the destitute and vulnerable, and we ask that You help these students and their families in powerful ways as only You can.

- According to Your Word in Malachi 4:6, we cry out that the hearts of the fathers be turned to their children and the hearts of the children be turned to their fathers. We pray for those parents who simply lack the motivation, sense of responsibility or the parenting skills to raise their children well. Break off apathy or helplessness and show them where they can find help. Please bring good parenting role models into the lives of young parents or teen moms who may not have had them while growing up.

- We lift up those parents who are doing their best but may be having to work two jobs, or who are single or divorced and living apart from their children, etc., and are simply unable to be present with them as much as they would like. Pour out Your grace on them, provide Your comforting presence to the children. Draw the parents to seek You for provision of creative ideas and resources to enable them to be the strong forces in their children's lives they want to be.

- Raise up effective spiritual fathers and mothers, we pray! Bring positive, godly role models into the lives of children who need them, including grandparents, aunts and uncles, coaches, Sunday school teachers, youth leaders, and others. Give these adults a heart to invest in the next generation.

Day 10: TEACHERS

Not many of you should become teachers, my
fellow believers, because you know that we
who teach will be judged more strictly.
(JAMES 3:1, NIV)

A servant of the Lord must not quarrel but must be kind to
everyone, be able to teach, and be patient with difficult people.
(2 TIMOTHY 2:24, NLT)

The quality of the teacher has a HUGE impact on how much students learn. Good teachers have an extraordinarily powerful impact on the future lives of their students. Similarly, there can be lasting damage that poor teachers can inflict on the lives of their students.

Furthermore, students who get the best teachers learn a lot—and students who get the worst teachers fall behind. There is widespread agreement that teachers matter most in producing educational results—more than class size, the curriculum, or the amount of money spent per student.

Sadly, there is a growing teacher shortage in the U.S. When indicators of teacher quality (certification, relevant training, experience, etc.) are taken into account, the shortage is even more acute, with high-poverty schools suffering the most from the shortage of credentialed teachers. Lack of sufficient, qualified teachers and staff instability threaten students' ability to learn and reduce teachers' effectiveness. High teacher turnover consumes valuable economic resources that could be better spent elsewhere.[9]

---

9. https://www.epi.org/publication/the-teacher-shortage-is-real-large-and -growing-and-worse-than-we-thought-the-first-report-in-the-perfect -storm-in-the-teacher-labor-market-series/. Accessed 27 February 2022.

Teachers are leaving for a variety of reasons. In some parts of the country, many are still facing rigid regulations related to the COVID-19 pandemic, and are growing discouraged as they see the children suffering under the restrictions and fear-and-control-based messaging. Some teachers, who know the danger and destruction that comes with the divisive and sometimes immoral curriculums they are being forced to teach, struggle to know how to exercise their faith and conscience. (Then, there are the teachers who are actively in support of these measures, whom we might even call "activist teachers," as noted on Day 6. They need our prayers, too, that the Holy Spirit would open their minds and hearts to the Truth.)

This shortage means that principals, superintendents, and counselors (and sometimes even parents!) are filling in as substitutes in classrooms that are struggling with staffing. This issue has been exacerbated by the COVID-19 "Omicron variant" infection surge, teachers' fears of becoming infected, and vaccination mandates. Where schools are holding the line on in-person learning, getting through the school day has required an "all-hands-on-deck" approach. In a school year where school teachers are being asked to help students recover academically and socially from the pandemic, some say they are dealing with overwhelming stress just trying to keep classes running.

This is a tumultuous time to be a schoolteacher. They need our support, encouragement, and prayers more than ever!

NOTE: If you know teachers, please pray for them by name.

Let's Pray

- Father, we are deeply grateful for our nation's schoolteachers! Thank You for their willingness to serve the next generation and for the personal sacrifice so many make as they go above and beyond the call of duty on behalf of their students.
- Lord, raise up more teachers who will see the education field as a ministry field. Increase the supply of educators with godly,

qualified individuals who have a passion for learning and for the next generation. Bring alongside them qualified volunteers, parents, and support staff who will make their job easier.

- Please streamline the workload of our teachers. Help them prioritize what is most important, and remove bureaucratic barriers that may prevent them from teaching at their best.

- We pray for any teacher who is exhausted from the day-to-day job stress and has lost vision and enthusiasm. Fulfill Your Word, that You "fully satisfy the needs of those who are weary and fully refresh the souls of those who are faint" (Jer. 31:25). We ask that You refresh and encourage those teachers who may be so discouraged that they are on the verge of leaving.

- We bless our teachers in the name of the Lord and ask for health and Your abundant blessing on their families, and most of all that they would know and serve You. Keep our teachers safe and keep them healthy.

- Holy Spirit, You are the ultimate Teacher, and we invite You into our classrooms and online learning experiences to lead students and teachers alike "into all truth." We lift up to You those teachers whose hearts and minds are not aligned with Your Truth, and who are actively engaged in turning their students away from You and from godly principles. We pray they would not be successful in this, and that they would come to a knowledge of the Truth and of the love and salvation of Jesus Christ.

- We declare that our teachers are loved and appreciated. They are not taken for granted. Hold them close as they help raise the next generation. Let them know how much they are valued as they leave a positive impact on this world.

Day 11: SUPPORT STAFF

And do not forget to do good and to share with others,
for with such sacrifices God is pleased.
(HEBREWS 13:16, NIV)

In the same way, let your light shine before others, that they
may see your good deeds and glorify your Father in heaven."
(MATTHEW 5:16, NIV)

Our school systems rely heavily on a vast army of crucial workers who make life and education happen for our children. These include para-educators and classroom assistants, librarians, counselors, tutors and specialists, school nurses, lunchroom and kitchen staff, school bus drivers, playground monitors, crossing and security staff, custodial staff, office workers, and more. When these positions are not well-funded, well-appreciated, and not filled with the highest quality of personnel, our children and their education suffer in many ways.

Particularly as they recover from pandemic-related learning and social issues, many children are dealing with a variety of potential stressors and, in many cases, their schools lack the resources to help them. Currently in the United States, the average student-to-school-counselor ratio is a whopping 464 to 1, according to the American School Counselor Association. Nearly 1 in 5 students—about 8 million—don't have access to a school counselor at all, with nearly 3 million of those students also lacking access to school psychologists, social workers, or any other type of support staff.[10]

These people fill vital roles in our schools and in our students' lives. We need to pray there are enough qualified support staff to adequately serve our children well.

---

10. https://parents-together.org/school-counselor-shortage-how-it-affects-your-children/. Accessed 27 February 2022.

Let's Pray

- Thank You, Lord, for this army of vital workers that often goes unnoticed and unappreciated in the roles they play. These people are the glue that holds together our schools. We pray they would experience Your pleasure and blessing on their sacrifices and investment in the lives of students.

- We ask You to provide the funding needed for support programs. So many of these positions are the first to be "cut" when there are budget shortfalls. Direct administrators to use finances wisely—and avoid the waste that frequently occurs—so that all available monies can be utilized effectively for these important staffing needs.

- Perhaps more than any other support staff, counselors have the greatest impact on students' lives, influencing strategic decisions involving education, career, relationships, and morality. We pray for more qualified Christian school counselors and psychologists in our schools, who will have godly values and a biblical worldview.

- Please protect the support staff personnel in every way: financially, physically, their health, their emotional well-being, and their family life. For all the vital qualities and programs they contribute, we pray You would use them to bring wisdom, guidance, creativity, safety, nutrition, health, and order.

- May they be governed by integrity and honor and kindness in all their interactions with students and one another. Help them to always treat students with dignity, respect, and compassion. We pray that they will experience satisfaction and significance in their jobs, and we ask You to use them in a mighty and powerful way in the lives of the students they serve.

Day 12: PRINCIPALS AND ADMINISTRATORS

First of all, then, I urge that supplications, prayers,
intercessions, and thanksgivings be made for all people, for
kings and all who are in high positions, that we may lead a
peaceful and quiet life, godly and dignified in every way.
(1 TIMOTHY 2:1-2, ESV)

The wisdom that comes from God is first utterly
pure, then peace-loving, gentle, approachable, full of
tolerant thoughts and kindly actions, with no breath
of favoritism or hint of hypocrisy. And the wise are
peace-makers who go on quietly sowing for a harvest
of righteousness—in other people and in themselves.
(JAMES 3:17-18, PHILLIPS)

Principals and administrators play a huge role in the education of our students. Their leadership sets the pace and priorities for schools. At the same time, many principals and vice principals are dealing with discipline issues with students, personnel issues with faculty and staff, and policy issues with the school district. School administrators "wear a lot of hats."

School district officials and administrators also play a key role as the bridge between state legislators and the communities they serve, making curricular choices, establishing and enforcing boundaries, setting policy, including regulating sports and extra-curricular policies, and other important decision-making responsibilities.

Of late, they are dealing with upset, even irate, parents who are fed up with the direction our education system is headed. Some of these administrators share the parents' concerns. Others actively resist them, siding with the progressive agenda. There is a lot of tension in school administration, and our principals and administrators bear much of the burden.

Let's Pray

Father, as taxpayers, voters, and parents we bring our educational system before You.

- We pray for those in authority over our schools, including principals, administrators, and education officials at every level. We pray for the Department of Education, the State Boards of Education, and County Education Agencies, and ask that You would bless all who work there.
- May Your wisdom direct them and may a fresh wind of Your Spirit blow into our state educational system at the highest levels! Where there is turmoil, we pray for peacemakers who can bring a fair and righteous outcome in a spirit of humility.
- We pray for the State Superintendents, and ask for the wisdom that is from above to be given to them: favor, strategy, and the ability to bring about consensus, cooperation, and reconciliation at the highest levels.
- We're grateful for all the district superintendents and school principals across the United States. Help them in their day-to-day responsibilities; let them function in a spirit of peace to bring peace and order into situations. Expand their leadership and executive abilities, we pray, and help them to implement innovative solutions to bring unity and productivity to their schools.
- Father, we will believe for positive and happy work environments and for healthy, professional regard and respect among all faculty, administration, and staff.
- We stand in faith and boldly declare that our nation's schools will embrace biblical values and operate on the principles of

our constitution and protect the rights of the weak and the "least of these," and that our rights of freedom of speech and freedom of religion will be upheld and protected in our classrooms and school districts this year.

- We declare that staff and faculty will not be antagonistic toward any Christian students or teachers and their values, but that You would change the hearts and minds of those who are offended by the gospel. Transform hostility into sincere inquiry and dialogue.
- May the hearts of all in leadership always put the good of our students first.

Day 13: SCHOOL BOARDS AND COMMUNITY SUPPORT

Let your light shine before men in such a
way that they may see your good works, and
glorify your Father who is in heaven.
(MATTHEW 5:16, NASB)

I showed you that by this kind of hard work we must
help the weak, remembering the words the Lord Jesus
himself said: "It is more blessed to give than to receive."
(ACTS 20:35, NIV)

Is not this the kind of fasting I have chosen . . . to share your
food with the hungry and to provide the poor wanderer
with shelter—when you see the naked, to clothe them,
and not to turn away from your own flesh and blood?
(ISAIAH 58:6-7, NIV)

S tudies show that local school boards play a critical role in the success of their district's schools. They have tremendous authority to make decisions at a local level including:

1. Strategic planning for their community's academic goals and establishing policies
2. Approving curricular materials
3. Being accountable to the community to make sure schools are well-run
4. Hiring and evaluating the district superintendent
5. Overseeing the budget, salaries for employees, and approving purchases

The role of school board members is one of the most important and influential in our community. School boards not only have a lasting impact on local education, they are typically the first step for anyone seeking higher public office as a mayor, state representative, or senator.

School boards are the launching pad for many political careers. If more Christian citizens were involved in their local school boards, it would not only be a blessing to our schools, but would also produce a strong pool of Christian candidates who would go on to win other local and state races. Think about the ways this could impact our communities, our states, and beyond!

(Of course, this highlights the importance of Christians being informed and VOTING in these critical elections! If just 10 percent more citizens with biblical values came out to vote, it would tip an election. In one case study in Austin, TX, for example, only 2.5 percent of registered voters showed up to the polls for one school board election! The study went on to say, *"Voters often do not know their elected school board members' names or responsibilities . . ."*)

Even if you are not a board member, as a concerned parent, property taxpayer, and a prayerful watchman, you can still attend school board meetings in your local area, get to know your board members, pray for them, and share your encouragement, ideas, or concerns.

Let's Pray

Heavenly Father, we lift up our school districts and boards to You and ask for Your leadership and wisdom to be present with them as they make decisions for our schools:

- For our local school boards, we pray that Your plans and purposes for each district and school would be reflected in their long-term strategic planning, and we invite Your Spirit to be present in every school board meeting across our state.
- We pray that godly people in our communities would step forward to run for the school board and take the place of leadership in this critical junction in our nation's history as we fight for truth at all levels of our society—particularly education.
- Lord, we pray for Your answers to the obstacles that often confront our school boards: the lack of unified vision, little urgency to implement needed reforms, resistance to change, frequent member turnover making it difficult to follow through on long-term strategies, financial shortfalls, community apathy, disunity, and a lack of stable leadership. We pray that You would bring order, peace, and clarity in these situations.
- When confronted with issues that clearly violate their conscience and the Word of God, we pray that You would empower school board members to stand up for what is right. We break off the spirit of intimidation and release Your power, love, and sound mind over them (2 Timothy 1:7) to stand up for truth and real justice.
- Lord, impart vision to the business community and to the elected representatives of the community as they partner

with their districts. We pray that local businesses would be moved to donate and support long-term programs in struggling schools. We pray for abundant funding to be released over schools and for the prospering of students and teachers.

- We ask for a new level of generosity and faith as churches and local organizations step up to provide food, clothing, and supplies for students. Give these organizations creative wisdom and strategies as they approach schools and distribute the resources that You are providing.

- Raise up Christians to partner with local schools in caring for the needs of every student and their families. Send godly volunteers, mentors, tutors, and coaches to come alongside students, teachers, and their families. We declare that Your Church will shine brightly and glorify God in our schools through unprecedented acts of love, service, and kindness, in Jesus' name!

Day 14: THE CHURCH

Then he said to his disciples, "The harvest is plentiful, but the laborers are few; therefore, pray earnestly to the Lord of the harvest to send out laborers into His harvest."
(MATTHEW 9:37-38, ESV)

"And now, Lord, take note of their threats, and grant that Your bondservants may speak Your word with all confidence, while You extend Your hand to heal, and signs and wonders take place through the name of Your holy servant Jesus." And when they had prayed, the place where they had gathered together was shaken, and they were all filled with the Holy Spirit and began to speak the word of God with boldness.
(ACTS 4:29-31, NASB)

Churches can support students both by what they provide for ministry within the church family, and how they invest time and energy into their surrounding local schools. Through traditional Sunday school ministry, summer VBS/sports camps/day camps, youth groups, mission trips, and more, the Church has a golden opportunity to minister to children and teens. The leaders of these ministries desperately need our prayers—and our hands-on involvement and support!

Many churches and Christian ministries have found that reaching out to their local schools is an important way to reach children and their families for Christ, as well as to strengthen ties with their communities. Prayer is also a huge and vital step to that engagement. There are also myriad ways that believers can support and invest in schools and help build God's Kingdom there.

You can get to know your public school officials and teachers by name. Thank them and express appreciation for the hard work they do. Send notes and cards of appreciation to teachers in your schools. Provide modest gifts as a token of appreciation, such as coffee shop or bookseller gift cards, plants, note pads, etc. Ask how you can pray for them, and really listen. Consider volunteering in a local school and being "boots on the ground" for bringing transformation and the light of Jesus to the campus.

Our communities' teachers need our tangible help. Reach out to the teachers you know and find out how you can be of service. Most importantly, pray—and then be a part of the transformation you are praying for! Churches, Christian ministries, and individual believers can build vital bridges of hope that can lead to stronger schools all across our state and nation.

Let's Pray

Thank You, Lord, for Your prophetic promise that we are on the verge of the greatest revival and spiritual awakening ever . . . and that America still has the opportunity to see the glory of God and another Great Awakening as seen in earlier centuries. As we stand in faith before You for these promises, we obey Your command to pray fervently that You would send workers into our schools and universities where the harvest indeed is plentiful.

- Thank You for the Christian leaders You have placed in our churches who faithfully teach Sunday school, lead VBS, organize summer camps and after-school programs, and who serve as youth group leaders. We pray You would bless them, energize them, and fill them with creative ideas and passion to continue to reach the next generation for Christ. They are helping train the next generation of Christian leaders!

- Thank You, too, for every Christian educator, para-educator, support staff, and administrator You have placed in our schools. We pray You would stir them up and help them resolve that this coming school year they will get to know You in a deeper way. May they walk more closely with You, be an example of godly character and righteousness, and show Your love and compassion to those around them.

- We fervently pray You would awaken the "sleeping giant" of Your Church, and that believers would become actively engaged in children's and youth ministries, their local schools, and our education system. Help us see this harvest field in our own backyards and find meaningful ways to serve and reach the next generation. Especially during this time of great need, when there is so much uncertainty, fear, isolation, and hopelessness, the Church has a message of hope to impart to our communities and schools. Show us how to do that!

- We pray for the young student evangelists in our schools. We ask for You to remove all fear of their peers, and any compromise and intimidation. We pray they would walk in an anointing to preach the gospel with power, and that they would see a flood of undeniable healings and miracles when they pray for others. Show them creative ideas to reach out to their classmates with the message of hope and love in Jesus.

- Thank You for the Christian students who will step into leadership roles with their peers during this time. We bless them and ask for a deep spiritual maturity, unshakeable courage, the zeal of the Lord, and that You would not let them be distracted from their high calling in You.

- May thousands of young leaders spring up from across our state, students who are wise beyond their years, faithful to the truth, and effective apologists for the gospel. Release the fivefold ministry (Ephesians 4:11) in our schools, we pray: the leaders, the pastors, the teachers, the prophets, and the evangelists!

SPIRITUAL AWAKENING

Preparing the Way for Hope, Healing, and Freedom

Day 15: SHIFTING THE SPIRITUAL ATMOSPHERE

"For I will pour out water on the thirsty
land and streams on the dry ground;
I will pour out My Spirit on your offspring
and My blessing on your descendants;
And they will spring up among the grass,
like poplars by streams of water."
(ISAIAH 44:3-4, NASB)

It's been a rocky couple of years in schools, filled with unprecedented and confusing changes and rules for students across the globe, heated protests by parents, large numbers of teachers leaving their jobs because of pandemic-related teaching challenges or refusing vaccine mandates, and crushing restrictions on the children themselves. No one knows with certainty what will happen in the days to come, but our prayer is that God will bring peace and calm to students in this new reality.

This year, students may be needing additional spiritual, mental, and emotional support (in addition to academics). They may feel extra shy, anxious, or unsure of their environment. For two years they have been hearing all kinds of talk of vaccines, variants, masking, and quarantines. While some states, counties, and districts are moving away from these measures, others are still experiencing them in various degrees. Parents may be worrying about their student's growth and emotional and academic well-being, as well as fear for their health.

The school climate for our students is still tenuous. Our prayers will aim to shift that climate of uncertainty for our students, starting with the spiritual atmosphere.

Let's begin our prayer focus with inviting the transforming presence of God's Spirit into our schools during this upcoming school year—to drive out any fear and uncertainty and replace it with a climate of peace and joy, one where our children will thrive and flourish. In an atmosphere that trusts God and welcomes His peace and presence, our children will be able to overcome the obstacles and reach their full God-given potential.

Let's Pray

Father, thank You for this incredible promise—that You will refresh the driest places!

- Where the environment has been spiritually dry and cold in our schools, we ask for streams of the Holy Spirit, the Water of Life, to pour into their hallways and classrooms.
- Where there is fear and uncertainty, we declare in Jesus' name there will be peace, confidence, and stability.
- We believe You will rain down an outpouring of Your presence that will shift the spiritual atmosphere on every school campus in our state, and cause our children to thrive and flourish like strong trees growing by the riverside.
- We ask for an unprecedented, tangible presence of the Holy Spirit in our schools, displacing the darkness and flooding the atmosphere of the classrooms with Your goodness and power!
- We pray that Christian students would be emboldened to share their faith in You, and courageous in their witness despite any opposition. Let them see undeniable demonstrations of Your power that will strengthen their faith.

- Empower all Christians there—students, teachers, and administrators—to truly be light and salt, in Jesus' name. We ask that You touch them so powerfully that they would acknowledge publicly that they belong to You.

Day 16: IDENTITY AND PURPOSE IN GOD'S DESIGN

We have not ceased to pray for you and to ask that you may be filled with the knowledge of His will in all spiritual wisdom and understanding, so that you will walk in a manner worthy of the Lord, to please Him in all respects, bearing fruit in every good work and increasing in the knowledge of God.
(COLOSSIANS 1:9-10, NASB)

Our children and young adults are desperately looking for identity and purpose, asking questions like: *Who am I? What makes me different? What is my purpose in this world?* In fact, in America, our children and youth are experiencing an identity *crisis*. Due to the pressure and messaging of the media—including social media like Instagram, Facebook, Snapchat, Tik Tok, and the like—young people often have no idea who they are, and feel compelled to try to be someone else. Oftentimes, what they see on social media tells them they're not good enough—that their clothes, their home, their car, and even their bodies need to be different or better.

Our identity is the first thing God establishes about us—we are made in God's image. Each of us is known by our Father God, who has a design for our lives within His perfect plan. However, evil forces are distorting the very core identity of our children—confusing them through the lie that they can decide who they want to be based on "feeling," instead of living out God's original design. A lot of false information about identity, sexuality, and life purpose is being disseminated through our public schools and greater society.

God's Word tells us that we have divinely powerful weapons for the tearing down of strongholds, and every lofty thing raised up against the truth of God (2 Corinthians 10:4-5). Prayer is one of those weapons we can use to tear down the strongholds of insignificance, inferiority, rejection, and comparison—and replace them with affirmation of and confidence in God's unconditional love and acceptance. Our students are valued by Him no matter what.

Let's Pray

Lord, thank You for Your promise to bless our children. Because of Your blessing, our children will find their true identity and sense of purpose in belonging to You, their Father and Creator.

- Please silence the negative voices telling our students they are worthless or unwanted, or that they can find their identity and purpose outside of Your plan for their lives. You have a unique design and plan for every student. We ask for these plans to be preserved, to give them a future and a hope! (Jer. 29:11)
- Almighty God, we pray for our future leaders; raise up young people with godly purpose and destiny to contend for the future of our nation! May many great young leaders like Moses, Joseph, Joshua, Daniel, Ruth, and Esther arise from our schools to bring justice and truth to every sector of society.
- Raise up those who will lead the way for truth in every mountain of influence: in government, in education, in media, in entertainment and the arts, in business and finance, in families, and in the Church. May they fulfill the purpose of God in their generation. Like David, may they know their calling from a young age, that no amount of family negativity, peer

pressure, or setbacks would discourage them from pursuing it. You have a plan for them that leads to life and fullness of joy.

- We pray for a revelation of TRUTH to our children about who they really are in You, and for protection for our children from false information about their purpose, sexuality, and Your design for life. We ask You to raise up spiritual watchmen (fathers, mothers, teachers, school leaders) who will watch, pray, and be a voice for truth in our schools.
- We declare, in Jesus' name, that this will be a year of blessing, revelation, refreshing, and new identity in God's original design for each student.

Day 17: IN ELEMENTARY SCHOOLS

Jesus called the children to him and said, "Let the
little children come to me, and do not hinder them,
for the kingdom of God belongs to such as these."
(LUKE 18:16, NIV)

Elementary school is a pivotal point in the lives of our children. They are young, often anxious about their first school experience, and very impressionable. For many kids, elementary school can be their first exposure to bullying, teasing, cliques, and other cruel behavior. It may also be their first exposure to extreme behavior such as major tantrums and violent outbursts, which have become rampant in our elementary schools. For some kids, elementary school is their first experience away from mom and dad, which may be tempting for them to "experiment" with behaviors that do not align with who they are.

Additionally, as our state and nation begin to recover from the COVID-19 pandemic, elementary-aged students are some of the most vulnerable. Social-emotional learning is paramount in their education, and being separated from their peers or having certain activities restricted (or even prohibited) can drastically impact their learning experience and psychological health.

We have the opportunity to lay foundations in children's lives through prayer, for them to be reassured, protected, and affirmed, and for a plumbline of truth, justice, and confidence to be laid in them—a foundation that will last a lifetime.

Let's Pray

Thank You, Lord, for Your heart of love and concern, especially for our youngest children! We pray for every young student in America, as well as their teachers and aides. The Kingdom of God belongs to them, even as Your Word says.

- We ask that these tender young hearts and minds would keep their innocence and purity. We pray that You would raise up an army of godly Christian teachers who are divinely gifted and called to teach and mold this impressionable age group.
- We pray for all of the social and emotional needs of our young students to be met. We pray that their hearts would be full of joy, and their elementary school experience would be uplifting, despite the circumstances.
- Pour out Your Spirit on these young ones, we pray! Let there be an awakening of their spirits and minds to You. May each student in America feel and see Your presence in their lives. May all of our children and the adults who teach and lead them encounter Your love and truth in a supernatural way!

Day 18: IN HIGH SCHOOLS

Even a child makes himself known by his acts,
by whether his conduct is pure and upright.
(PROVERBS 20:11, ESV)

Blessed are those whose way is blameless,
who walk in the law of the Lord!
Blessed are those who keep his testimonies,
who seek him with their whole heart,
who also do no wrong, but walk in his ways! You have
commanded your precepts to be kept diligently. Oh, that
my ways may be steadfast in keeping your statutes!
(PSALM 119:1-5, ESV)

High school can be an incredibly intense time for teens, as they navigate dating and romantic relationships, friendship struggles, identity crises, bullying, exposure to drugs, alcohol, sex, immense peer pressure, and much more. It's no wonder that almost 70 percent of Christian youth leave the Church after high school. It's one of the most volatile seasons of life for young people, and we must pray to cover our nation's high schools with God's presence.

It's important for young people to know that "Christian life" can and does exist beyond chapels, church youth groups, and worship services. It is our deepest hope that the teens of America would discover the multitude of ways they can bring Christian life to their circle of friends and high school campus. Through clubs, prayer groups, and being open with their faith testimony with peers, high schools can become thriving hosts for spiritual impact and transformation. There are many ways teens can connect, communicate, and even gather to share and experience Christ together. We pray for boldness among the Christian teens in our communities, that they would bring more of their friends into the Kingdom of God on the mission field of their high school relationships.

At the same time, high school is ripe with temptation. There are daily spiritual battles taking place for our teens' purity, tempting them to believe that they must grow up sooner than they really should. We must also pray against all forces that would tell them they need to drink, party, or sleep around in order to experience acceptance. We pray in Jesus' name that all high school students would discover their worth and wholeness in the eyes of Christ, and not in the eyes of the world or their peers.

Let's Pray

God, first and foremost, we pray for a great turnaround in the statistic that 70 to 75 percent of Christian youth leave the Church after high school. Heavenly Father, we ask You to intervene in our young people's lives and break this trend. Bring Your answers to parents, churches, and Christian schools! In Jesus' name, keep our children close to You as they navigate the pressures of teenagehood.

- We pray for godly teachers and school administrators to guide high schoolers with truth and love.
- Among our students we ask for edifying and fulfilling friendships, rather than negative influences that would cause them to turn from You.
- Our alternative high schools have unique student populations that are usually experiencing even higher levels of brokenness and challenges. (Many times, these students are trying to overcome significant adversities and roadblocks to education, and may be dealing with juvenile incarceration, housing insecurity, pregnancy and parenting, addictions, and more, in even greater numbers than in regular high schools.) We pray You would give extra strength and grace to the teachers

and administrators of these students. Pour out Your mercy on these children and give them Your Spirit to help them overcome their adversity and go on to know You, follow You, and achieve success in their lives.

- We bind the spirits that lead teens in all of our schools into partying, substance abuse, and provocative behavior. Lord, cover our students in a hedge of Your protection. Cause them to feel a wholeness and acceptance that only comes from Your unfailing love for them.

- May the Christian students in all of our high schools walk in boldness, proudly proclaiming Your name. Anoint them with a bravery that only comes from You. We declare victory over all spirits that would bind our students in fear, preventing them from sharing openly about their faith. We pray against the fear of man, the fear of rejection, or any other trepidation that would make them feel anxious about sharing their testimony. May there be a wave of spiritual awakening in our high schools that sweeps across our state and our nation!

Day 19: IN COLLEGES AND UNIVERSITIES

*"Have I not commanded you? Be strong and courageous.
Do not be frightened, and do not be dismayed, for
the Lord your God is with you wherever you go."*
(JOSHUA 1:9, NIV)

*"O LORD, I give my life to you. I trust in you,
my God! Do not let me be disgraced,
or let my enemies rejoice in my defeat. No one
who trusts in you will ever be disgraced,
but disgrace comes to those who try to deceive
others. Show me the right path, O LORD;*

point out the road for me to follow. Lead
me by your truth and teach me,
for you are the God who saves me. All
day long I put my hope in you."
(PSALM 25:1-5, NLT)

Today, college campuses serve a highly strategic purpose in the life of our nation. Not only are all of a nation's future leaders gathering to be trained and commissioned, but even the best and brightest from the nations of the world are being sent to our colleges and universities!

But there is a crisis on our college campuses today: they are in dire need of the presence of God! The reality is that many universities are not only training future leaders into occupational roles; they are also systematically shaping hearts and minds into a worldview devoid of God. The effects have been devastating on a generation. The very places that once trained young people in the Word of God are now the very places where most young people lose their faith.

The statistics support these observations; the emotional and mental health of college students has become a growing concern. According to a recent national survey, 95 percent of counseling center directors expressed increasing concern by the numbers of students "with significant psychological problems" and 70 percent indicated an increase in the numbers of students with severe psychological problems from the previous year.[11] Anxiety is the top presenting concern (41.6 percent), followed by depression (36.3 percent) and relationship problems (35.8 percent).[12]

---

11. "College Students' Mental Health a Growing Concern, Survey Finds." *American Psychological Association.* Published June 2013, Vol. 44, No. 6. Page 13.

12. "Depression and Anxiety Among College Students" by Margarita Tartakovsky, M.S. Published October 8, 2018. https://psychcentral.com/lib /depression-and-anxiety-among-college-students. Accessed June 25, 2019.

Additionally, according to Addiction Center, "College students make up one of the largest groups of drug abusers nationwide, and are "twice as likely to abuse drugs and alcohol than those who don't attend college."[13]

Yet, there is hope. In similar times in our nation's history, when darkness has overtaken our colleges and universities, and when God's people have united in faith to pray for the outpouring of God's Spirit on colleges, He has responded to revive a generation! God has done it before; let's ask Him to do it again!

Let's Pray

Father, we pray today for our colleges and universities, that they would be filled with the tangible presence of God.

- Father, we pray for a movement of holiness, righteousness, and purity on the college campuses of America—that will cause the student body to be washed clean by the blood of Jesus (1 John 1:7; Heb. 9:14)! We pray for a revelation of the beauty of Your holiness (Ps. 27:4; 29:2), that they would desire to seek You and honor You above all, to turn away from all sin, and to be holy as You are holy (1 Pet. 1:15-16).

- Lord, we ask You to break off every addiction to alcohol, drugs, pornography, and sexual immorality among the student body and the faculty. We ask for the power of Your Spirit within hearts to renounce all agreements with destructive lifestyles and sin patterns, and to find complete freedom, cleansing and healing by the blood of Jesus!

- We declare a turning in the hearts of students and faculty, to willingly offer their bodies as living sacrifices, holy and

13. "College Students and Drug Abuse." *AddictionCenter*, an informational web guide by Recovery Worldwide. https://www.addictioncenter.com /college. Accessed June 24, 2019.

pleasing to You (Rom. 12:1-2). Uproot the lies that they are unable to break free. By Your power, break off every soul tie, every addiction, and every deception that would try to hold their souls captive to their own desires.

- Lord, we pray each student will have the opportunity to grow and develop spiritually as well as intellectually, and that they would be grounded in the truth. Instead of their courses and higher learning pulling them away from their faith in God, we pray students will be brought closer to You.

- We thank You for those students who are courageously living their faith and displaying it on campus. Give our Christian students courage to live out their faith in an atmosphere that is often skeptical of faith.

- Lord, we lift up the professors, deans, and presidents of our colleges. We ask that they not only be wise in their area of specialty, but also that You give them spiritual wisdom. We pray that the Holy Spirit will use Christian professors and faculty as a mighty force for truth and that a new standard of righteousness would be raised up on our campuses.

- We ask for an all-consuming hunger and desperation for Your presence on our college and university campuses, that only You can give—that students would desire You more than anything else in this life! Let nothing else satisfy them but the presence of God, touching an entire generation!

- Only You can heal the brokenness that runs so deep within our campuses, Lord. Only You can restore the years the enemy has stolen from this generation. More than anything else You could give us, we ask for this one thing: that our young people might behold You all the days of their lives and dwell in Your presence (Ps. 27:4)! May they experience the fullness of Your presence—heaven on earth!

- We declare that our colleges and universities will become centers for truth and revival, rather than for the tearing down of the faith of our young adults. We ask You to work through Christian groups and churches on campuses to bring thousands of young men and women to faith in Jesus Christ.

Day 20: IN HOMESCHOOLS AND CHRISTIAN SCHOOLS

God gave these four young men an unusual aptitude for understanding every aspect of literature and wisdom.
(DANIEL 1:17, NLT)

You have been taught the Holy Scriptures from childhood, and they have given you the wisdom to receive the salvation that comes by trusting in Christ Jesus.
(2 TIMOTHY 3:15, NLT)

My prayer is not that you take them out of the world but that you protect them from the evil one.
(JOHN 17:15, NIV)

There are many reasons why parents choose to send their children to private school or to keep them at home to educate them. Many times it is because they want to have greater opportunity to instill biblical values or pursue a certain emphasis in the children's education. In some cases, children with special needs are not being served adequately by the local public school district. Many parents have chosen to homeschool because of the uncertainty caused by COVID-19, others because they have become aware of the unprecedented assaults on truth and biblical values their children are facing in the classroom.

For these reasons and others, homeschooling rates within the United States are higher than they have been in decades. Between 2019 and 2021, homeschooling rates more than doubled.[14]

Some families in the United States have created a modern version of the one-room schoolhouse, sometimes called "homeschooling pods." Under this model, a small group of parents split the cost of hiring teachers and tutors and paying for resources such as online classes. Founded in 2015, a program of this nature called Outschool has seen a 30-fold increase in enrollment since the start of the current pandemic.

Whatever the reason parents may choose to utilize them, homeschools and private schools are extremely important components of our states' educational opportunities, and we want to pray for parents and teachers as they undertake this valuable endeavor.

Let's Pray

Lord, we thank You for every private Christian school, college, preschool, and every godly homeschool in our state. Thank You for the parents, teachers, and families who are hard at work educating the next generation in excellence and with a biblical worldview.

- As You did for Solomon and for Daniel, please give our Christian students maturity beyond their years and a supernatural ability to learn and to excel academically, above and beyond the norm.

- We invite Your manifest presence to come to these classrooms and homes and ask for a great move of God among these

---

14. Bureau, U. S. C. (2021, March 22). *Homeschooling on the Rise During COVID-19 Pandemic.* The United States Census Bureau. https://www.census.gov/library/stories/2021/03/homeschooling-on-the-rise-during-covid-19-pandemic.html.

students, parents, and teachers! We pray for true revival to come to our Christian schools with a great outpouring of the Holy Spirit that would impact every family.

- We ask You, Jehovah Jireh, for a great financial blessing to come to each of these and pray that You would reward and bless them for their commitment and sacrifice: to the teacher in a Christian school with a significantly smaller paycheck, to the student paying tuition fees, and to the parent who experiences a loss of income to stay home and teach their children.

- Many of our Christian schools and colleges face financial challenges and we ask for dramatic financial breakthroughs for each of them! Protect these institutions from negative press designed to pressure them into compromising their stand for the gospel and righteousness. We pray for their governing boards to make decisions in the fear of the Lord and with great wisdom, and that You would guide them in the days ahead.

- Father, we fervently cry out to You for every Christian student in our schools, no matter their school or age. We ask that even our youngest Christian children would be taught Your truth from childhood, and that they would have a deep understanding of the Bible. Send them teachers and pastors who can impart an intelligent biblical worldview to them and disciple them into followers of You.

Day 21: RECLAIM A GENERATION

". . . that they may be called oaks of righteousness,
the planting of the LORD, that he may be glorified.

They shall build up the ancient ruins;
they shall raise up the former devastations;
they shall repair the ruined cities,
the devastations of many generations."
(ISAIAH 61:3B-4, ESV)

If we are to see revival in our day, and reformation in our lifetime, we must influence and regain control of the educational systems of our nation. A generation has very nearly been stolen from us, and must be reclaimed for the Kingdom of God. We need an invasion of prayer power and reformers into every facet of society if we are to see transformation and a Great Reformation occur!

Daniel and his friends Shadrach, Meshach, and Abednego were all young Hebrew men of excellence, trained in the ways of the Babylonians (Dan. 1:3-4). They took their training and skill and applied it, without compromise, to their secular surroundings. They were not distracted by the attractions and temptations of the affluent culture they found themselves in. Anointed and appointed by God, they experienced supernatural intervention and changed the course of a nation.

We need a godly generation to arise in our day, equipped and skilled in ways our culture will listen and respond to. This will be no simple task. While Christian influence in our school systems has been all but eradicated, secular humanists have been discipling our children into their belief system. Through their calculated efforts over many decades, humanists and atheists have commandeered our education system and used it to propagate their ideologies. As a result, a dark and evil anti-Christ force is currently dominating our school systems.

Yet we are not without hope! God's Word is full of promises for the children and grandchildren of the righteous:

> *"This is what the LORD says: 'Restrain your voice from weeping and your eyes from tears, for your work will be rewarded,' declares the LORD. 'They [your children] will return from the land of the enemy. So there is hope for your descendants,' declares the LORD."*
> (JER. 31:16-17, NIV)

> *"Be assured, an evil person will not go unpunished, but the offspring of the righteous will be delivered."*
> (PROV. 11:21, ESV)

> *"And all your [spiritual] children shall be disciples [taught by the Lord and obedient to His will], and great shall be the peace and undisturbed composure of your children."*
> (IS. 54:13, AMPC)

> *"Blessed are those who fear the LORD, who find great delight in his commands. Their children will be mighty in the land; the generation of the upright will be blessed."*
> (PSALM 112:1-2, NIV)

> *"For I will pour water on the thirsty land, and streams on the dry ground; I will pour out my Spirit on your offspring, and my blessing on your descendants."*
> (IS. 44:3, NIV)

> *"For thus says the LORD: 'Even the captives of the mighty shall be taken, and the prey of the tyrant be*

> *rescued, for I will contend with those who contend*
> *with you, and I will save your children.'''*
>
> (Is. 49:25, ESV)

For good or evil, the education system is a training ground for our young people. We cannot be silent or passive; we must get involved with our prayers and godly actions. If we are to see revival and reformation in our nation, we must raise up and equip a generation of young people like Daniel and his friends. We must claim the promises of God for the next generation, and pray He raises them up as reformers and world-changers!

Let's Pray

Father, we praise You that You have heard every prayer during these past 21 days as we have cried out to You on behalf of our students, teachers, families, and schools. We ask that You would be glorified, that You would be exalted over our schools and over every power and principality that would seek to influence and infiltrate our education system with the purpose to deceive and destroy the next generation.

- We ask You to bless the students in the preschools, home schools, alternative, private, charter, and public schools, and the colleges and universities of America with the Spirit of wisdom and revelation in the knowledge of You, Your Word, and Your Kingdom purposes.
- We declare it is time for our Christian students and teachers to ARISE AND SHINE as Your glory rises upon them, and that nations will come to the brightness of Your rising (Is. 60:1,3).
- We stand in faith on Your many prophetic promises that Your glory is going to be manifested on the earth in a dramatic and unprecedented way.

- Thank You that when You revealed Your glory to Moses, it was Your *goodness* that passed in front of him! Likewise, we remain confident knowing that we will surely see the goodness of the Lord in the land of the living (in our schools) (Psalm 27:13)!
- Reveal Yourself and Your ways in undeniable and sovereign acts. Empower and equip our children to fulfill their sovereign purpose according to the highest plans of God, in Jesus' name.
- Heavenly Father, Creator of all life, You have dreamed a unique dream for every individual. Therefore, we cry out and say, "The destinies of our children will be preserved!" Give this emerging generation vision and a sense of purpose regarding their future. Father God, it is time! Raise up sons and daughters with godly purpose and destiny to contend for the future of our nation (Is. 22:22). Raise up ones that will lead the way for righteousness and justice, in every mountain of cultural influence. May they, like David, fulfill the purpose of God in their generation (Acts 13:36).

APPENDIX

WAYS TO ENGAGE
THE CHURCH COMMUNITY

We encourage you to invite churches, families, youth groups, children's churches, and individuals to pray with you in an intentional and focused way as you lift up schools in your community to God. Make available this *Reclaim a Generation* prayer guide to help them pray.

Although there are so many issues that are plaguing our schools and our youth, we believe God is the solution to the most difficult of problems and wants to intervene in response to His people's prayers.

Ways to Engage Everyone

Select one or more schools that God lays on your heart and set aside time to pray specifically for that school, its issues, students, teachers, administrators, and district leaders.

We HIGHLY encourage that you prayerwalk or prayer drive several times a week around the perimeter of your chosen school. Prayerwalking or prayer driving near and around a school helps engage hearts to pray with more fervency and focus for the needs of the teachers and students.

Pastors/Churches

If you are a pastor or church leader, consider setting aside a weekend service to honor and pray for educators. Ask God's blessing over them and pray for empowerment to succeed and prosper throughout the school year.

Encourage your congregation to pray together as families for their children's schools. Create a special service to pray for ALL the schools in your area. Make it a time to pray for their young people, educators, and the school year as a whole. This could be a church-wide prayer meeting with every age participating and represented.

Select the nearest school or school district and pray for its principals and key leadership by name during the weekend service. Consider having church members form small groups to pray together.

On a Saturday during the 21 days, organize multiple church-wide prayerwalks near different school locations and set up coordinators for each prayerwalking team.

Youth Groups/Youth Pastors

Youth groups and youth pastors can set aside time at each of their youth services to pray for a different topic related to schools (friends by name, activities and clubs, their school leadership/administration, etc.)

They could organize prayerwalks around the perimeter of their students' schools one Saturday, engaging the whole youth group to target different schools TOGETHER.

TIPS FOR SCHOOL PRAYERWALKING

What is "prayerwalking"? Prayerwalking is talking with our Heavenly Father through His Son Jesus Christ while walking. Here, our focus is upon our neighborhood schools. Praying near a campus brings us in close proximity with our prayer target. We begin to see with the eyes and compassion of Jesus the needs of the young people for whom we are interceding.

Three components work together while prayerwalking:

1. *Worship.* Proclaim the excellencies of the name of Jesus or softly sing a song which exalts the Lord and His mighty power.
2. *Warfare.* Prayerwalking is spiritual battle. You may experience an indirect onslaught of the enemy: confusion or pestering of the mind, causing thoughts to wander or telling you this isn't doing any good. Press through these roadblocks. Realize that the Lord has given you authority over the evil one. Remember, that every place you walk, you have been given spiritual authority to restrain, limit, and displace evil forces (Luke 10:19; Josh. 1: 3).
3. *Welcome.* Invite God's transforming presence to permeate the school for which you are praying. Integrate these three "W's" in a good balance, though at times one or another may seem to be emphasized.

Do's and Don'ts of Prayerwalking

Do: Worship God as you prayerwalk or prayer drive the school's perimeter. Welcome God's Holy Spirit to the school for which you are praying. Pronounce blessings upon the teachers, students, and staff. Pray salvation, healing, and spiritual freedom for the students who attend there.

Don't: Draw attention to yourself. You have an audience of One—Jesus Christ. It would be best not to go on the campus during school hours since there is increased security at schools these days (go before or after school or on weekends).

In Preparation

It is important to prepare our mind, body, and spirit. You are about to become a bridge of blessing between heaven and earth! Don't allow any feelings of inadequacy to plague you. You have indicated your willingness by your presence, and God is always faithful to take us where we are and lead us. In prayer, there is no failure.

The book *Prayerwalking*, by Steve Hawthorne, offers the following tips to prepare for a prayerwalk:

1. **Start with vocalizing your praise to the Lord.** Whether you sing, shout, or whisper, warm up your vocal cords with praise before setting out. Put the name of Jesus on your lips. Seek to position your heart before God in fresh gratitude and blessing.
2. **Take charge of the directions your mind will go.** Fix your attention on the purposes and ways and thoughts of God before you launch out. If you find your mind wandering, read Scripture out loud.
3. **Seek God for guidance at intervals.** Then trust that He is guiding you!

4. **Take a few minutes to connect and pray with others on your prayer team.** Find out if anyone is sensing/hearing anything from the Lord.

5. **Take your stance before the Father.** Remember that you are positioned in heavenly places through the blood and authority of Jesus.

What to Do During the Prayerwalk

1. **Open your eyes.** Ask God to help you see with His eyes.

2. **Open your ears.** Listen for God's whispered cues. Expect Him to highlight truths you have hidden in your heart and apply them to what is around you. Practice silence as you listen to God's Spirit.

3. **Pray together.** Seek to consciously follow and reinforce prayers lifted by others on the prayer team.

4. **Pray with Scripture.** You can be confident of praying the will of God when you are praying His Word. God has breathed life into His Word and loves to bless it. He has promised that His Word will not return to Him void. Read it over and over again.

5. **Pray with Holy Spirit sensitivity** to the people and places you are actually encountering. Don't be surprised if the Lord guides you to focus and concentrate your prayers on some locations more than others.

What to Pray

Based upon Luke 11:2-4: "When you pray, say: 'Our Father in heaven, hallowed be your name. Your kingdom come. Your will be done on earth as it is in heaven. Give us day by day our daily bread. And forgive us our sins, for we also forgive everyone who is indebted to us. And do not lead us into temptation, but deliver us from the evil one.'" (Luke 11:2-4, NKJV)

1. **Pray for God's Glory.** Pray that God would work so that He would be honored, adored, lifted up, revealed and praised by name among our students and in our schools.

2. **Pray for God's Kingdom.** Pray with expectancy for heaven's liberating power to be released on the students and schools.

3. **Pray for reconciliation.** Ask God to reconcile every student to Himself. Ask God to bring reconciliation where there are offenses or breeches among students themselves, and among students and teachers.

4. **Pray for God to release His Spirit on the campus.** Pray He would lead all students, teachers, administrators, and support staff into the light of His love and truth, rescuing them from darkness and destruction and reclaiming them for the purposes of heaven.

Scriptures for Prayerwalking

(Note: All scriptures are from the NIV version.)

"Shout for joy to God, all the earth! Sing the glory of his name; make his praise glorious. "How awesome are your deeds! So great is your power that your enemies cringe before you. All the earth bows down to you; they sing praise to you, they sing the praises of your name." (Psalm 66:1-4)

"And they were calling to one another: 'Holy, holy, holy is the Lord Almighty; the whole earth is full of his glory.'" (Is. 6:3)

"May God be gracious to us and bless us and make his face shine on us so that your ways may be known on earth, your salvation among all nations. May the peoples praise you, God; may all the peoples praise you." (Psalm 67:1-3)

"A voice of one calling: 'In the wilderness prepare the way for the Lord; make straight in the desert a highway for our God. Every

valley shall be raised up, every mountain and hill made low; the rough ground shall become level, the rugged places a plain. And the glory of the Lord will be revealed, and all people will see it together. For the mouth of the Lord has spoken.'" (Is. 40:3-5)

"Let this be written for a future generation, that a people not yet created may praise the Lord: 'The Lord looked down from his sanctuary on high, from heaven he viewed the earth, to hear the groans of the prisoners and release those condemned to death.'" (Psalm 102:18-20)

"Rather, as it is written: 'Those who were not told about him will see, and those who have not heard will understand.'" (Romans 15:21)

"Teach me your way, Lord, that I may rely on your faithfulness; give me an undivided heart, that I may fear your name. I will praise you, Lord my God, with all my heart; I will glorify your name forever. For great is your love toward me; you have delivered me from the depths, from the realm of the dead." (Psalm 86:11-13)

"When you pray, say: 'Father, hallowed be your name, your kingdom come. Give us each day our daily bread. Forgive us our sins, for we also forgive everyone who sins against us. And lead us not into temptation.'" (Luke 11:2-4)

"I urge, then, first of all, that petitions, prayers, intercession and thanksgiving be made for all people, for kings and all those in authority, that we may live peaceful and quiet lives in all godliness and holiness. This is good, and pleases God our Savior, who wants all people to be saved and to come to a knowledge of the truth." (1 Timothy 2:1-4)

"He told them, 'The harvest is plentiful, but the workers are few. Ask the Lord of the harvest, therefore, to send out workers into his harvest field.'" (Luke 10:2)

ABOUT THE AUTHOR

 CHERYL SACKS is a best-selling author, national conference speaker, prayer mobilizer, and church prayer consultant. Her "Prayer-Saturated" series—including *The Prayer-Saturated Church* (NavPress/Tyndale), *Prayer-Saturated Kids* (NavPress/Tyndale), and *The Prayer-Saturated Family* (Chosen)— have blessed and mentored tens of thousands of individuals to go deeper into prayer, and have greatly impacted thousands of churches.

A former public school teacher and administrator, Cheryl's heart is to see a new generation of youth empowered to pray with purpose and passion, and to become reformers for the Kingdom of God in their spheres of influence. Cheryl and her husband, Hal, lead BridgeBuilders International, based in Phoenix, Arizona. They have a married daughter and three grandchildren.

Learn more about Hal and Cheryl Sacks' ministry at:
www.prayersaturated.life
www.bridgebuilders.net

 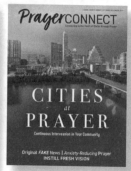 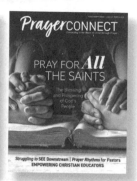